FALLING THROUGH LOVE

ALSO BY AKIF KICHLOO

The Feeling May Remain

Poems That Lose

FALLING THROUGH LOVE

poems

AKIF KICHLOO

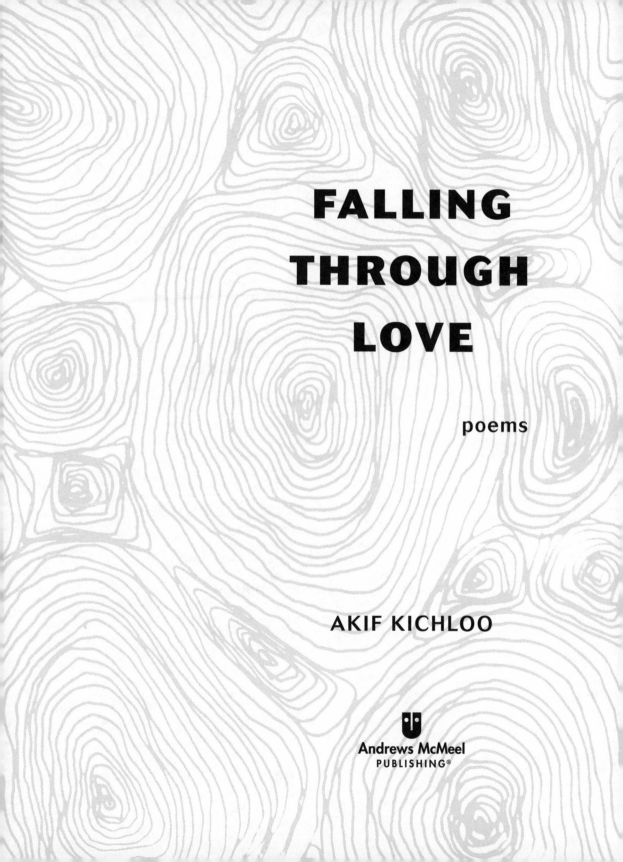

Andrews McMeel
PUBLISHING®

Andrews McMeel Publishing
a division of Andrews McMeel Universal
1130 Walnut Street, Kansas City, Missouri 64106

www.andrewsmcmeel.com

19 20 21 22 23 VEP 10 9 8 7 6 5 4 3 2 1

ISBN: 978-1-5248-5115-6

Library of Congress Control Number: 2019945069

Editor: Patty Rice
Art Director: Holly Swayne
Production Editor: Meg Daniels
Production Manager: Carol Coe

ATTENTION: SCHOOLS AND BUSINESSES
Andrews McMeel books are available at quantity discounts with bulk purchase for
educational, business, or sales promotional use. For information, please e-mail the
Andrews McMeel Publishing Special Sales Department:
specialsales@amuniversal.com.

CONTENTS

Acknowledgments

I am grateful to the following publications and their editors, where versions of these poems first found homes.

FlyPaper Magazine:　　　"Courage: Making Sure Your Mother Knows That Her Prayers Don't Work"

Homology Lit:　　　"Horrors of My Childhood Horrors,"
"My Father Says Poetry Will Not Pay My Bills, Clinical Practice Will"

Obra / Artifact:　　　"I Think You Have Heard This Before"

Kissing Dynamite:　　　"*Salam.* I Am Sorry for Yesterday," "Secretly I Am a Mathematician"

Nightingale & Sparrow:　　　"Dreamers Dream Dreamers Do"

Sheraza:　　　"Riptides of You"

Verse of Silence:　　　"Basta"

Palette Poetry:　　　"An Autumn Infinite"

My deepest gratitude to my elder brother, Asim Kichloo, and his wife, Farah Wani Kichloo, for allowing me to stay at their home for the final months of working on this book. This book wouldn't have been possible without their support.

To my sweetest nephew and best friend Adam, for all the exhilarating tales from his four-year-old existence and some real deep talk. For his honesty, innocence, and unconditional love. For making me believe in love again.

To Surbhi Pathania, for being there for me whenever I needed someone to look over new work and for contributing her wonderful artwork to this book. It wouldn't be the same without her help.

To the wonderful staff at Barnes & Noble, Saginaw, Michigan, for allowing me to sit on their couches for the better part of six months, and the baristas there, for refilling my coffee mugs an endless number of times, and, of course, those two-for-one cookies.

To everyone I crossed paths with while staying one full year at the foothills of Himalayas, in Himachal Pradesh, India, where this book was originally conceived.

To Dr. Asif Khan, for doing what he does best.

To Adnan Khateeb, for his ceaseless technical support.

And to every patron of the arts. Thank you. By supporting artists, you are helping make this world bearable enough for everyone to live in.

I wrote this book for everyone who has sacrificed something for passion and for love. And for everyone who has helped someone realize their dream.

> *"dukhiya jaage dukh de kaaran*
> *par sukhiya nah jaage koyi."*

> "it is the sorrows that keep the sorrowful awake
> but the joyful are not awake."

> —*Baba Bulleh Shah*

To the ones who got away
To the ones who stayed

(جو رہے اور جو چلے گئے۔)

"Live the questions now. Perhaps you will then
gradually, without noticing it, live along some distant
day into the answer."

—*Rainer Maria Rilke*

"Mela ee pal di pal ve
Chal mele noon challiye.
Aakhir jaana mar ve
Chal mele noon challiye."

"The sparkling assembly of this world is now here and now gone
Let's go and see its sights for these few moments.
We must ultimately die and leave here
Let's go and see its sights for these few moments."

—*Waris Shah*

FALLING THROUGH LOVE

Some days I am a lifesaver,
A blooming rosebud,
A liberated thought.
Some days all I am is
death.

I
———

AUTUMN INFINITE

Saccharine Calamity / Earthquake Being

My Father Says Poetry Will Not Pay My Bills, Clinical Practice Will

On the inside of my ribs, dreams flower into guilt,
turn into a familiar heaviness there is no getting used to.
My chest is nothing but fire, a dry-wood house that will burn
until all my desires are repressed. In my window,
the moon glitters, as if trembling with truth. Tonight,
to keep from dying, I bury myself in a poem.
The moon shirks in shame. Hides behind my father's
mountain of a shadow. During the day, the sun lights my sky.
My sweat lubricates pistons of some hereditary engine inside my limbs. I run
from room to room. Patient to patient. With my father egging me on, I cure
every illness my god has conjured. See, in my profession I correct
my god's wrongs. In my passion I wrong my father's right.
I don't know how this art came to me. I don't know when I became
everything I was never to be. But these words creep up on me, you know.
Jump out of dark allies and rob me of all comforts of the world.
I never see approval in my father's aging face. And I write a poem.
I never spot peace in my mother's beautiful eyes. And I write a poem.
My brother keeps forgetting my name. And. I write a poem.

I Think You Have Heard This Before

I am thinking of irreplaceable love   love filled with only love   a father
jumps back into a burning house to save his little boy   saves his
little boy   his lungs fill with soot until his lungs eat the soot   there is
an animal carcass on the road   plump as death   swollen
who of us will be an orphan today?   let me be careless with my words
coffins are being filled with people who were loved   when I said I can
cure the world the therapist said he can cure my world
let me describe to you a scene   a toddler is lying belly-down in his crib
the stuffed lion is roaring angrily on his back   the mother enters the scene
picks up both the toddler and the roaring lion on his back   puts the
toddler to her breast   the lion falls asleep.

Secretly I Am a Mathematician

(I)
Secretly I am a saint.
I fuck but *never* procreate.

Subtraction > Addition

When I was a child I found the trick to multiplication
$9 \times 1 = 10 - 1$
$9 \times 2 = 20 - 2$
$9 \times 3 = 30 - 3$
You see how subtraction is an easier pursuit.

(II)
When I started learning the Urdu alphabet *alif bay pay tay* (ا ب پ ت)
I always forgot to recall the letter پ (*pay*).
My father thrashed me so hard I screamed
alif bay pay tay, alif bay pay tay, alif bay pay tay, for weeks in my sleep.
Like a split heartbeat. A sound of disease. *alif bay pay tay, alif bay pay tay,*
alif bay pay tay.
Years later I learned the letter پ (*pay*) is absent in the Arabic language.
(If you have to write "Pepsi" in Arabic, you write "Bebsi" instead.)

You see   *Absence*   *Effortless to learn*
             Subtraction   *Easier*

(III)
Easy is سهل (*sahal*) in Arabic, Urdu, and Kashmiri
Which becomes آسان (*aasaan*) in Persian and Hindi (आसान)
Which becomes ਸੌਖਾ (*saukha*) in Punjabi and again اسانه (*āsāna*) in Pashto.
All seven languages my ancestors spoke at some point until
I subtracted them down to just one.

(IV)
Sick men are hung to
death because it is said that death
by hanging is death by humiliation.
Every time a man is hung by his neck, his manhood swells to an erection.
During partition so many men were hung all anyone ever saw
was floods.   *Do these look like additions?*

Millions of faces that never aged   *subtraction*
So many children growing up without fathers   *subtraction*
My father slapping me senseless   *unrelated but still subtraction.*

(V)
In our house there was a tradition
Children behaved like grown-ups and grown-ups behaved like children.
There is no way to remember how I felt the day I was born
but I cannot forget the day I couldn't place the letter پ *(pay)*   that day I ripened.

Salam. I Am Sorry for Yesterday

If I say I am sorry for yesterday, which yesterday
am I referring to? Anxiety mimes hysteria, hysteria
mimes past tragedies, and you become a ghost.
A sick imposter. Hiding. Scaring everybody back
to innocence. *Can you call it trauma if you can't
show the scars?* You learn to say your namastes,
fold your hands in gratitude, write your thank-yous
with sparkling brilliance, and apologize. Repeatedly
apologize.

Salam.
I am sorry for yesterday.
Allah Hafiz.

When Prophet Muhammad was kicked out of Mecca,
he made a kingdom on its outskirts, called it المدينة (*al-Madinah*),
called it "the city", called it "home". My mother pushed me out
at 10:30 p.m., on a hot, humid, summer day, on a government-
paid hospital bed, and she swears I didn't stop crying for two full
days. It was horrifying. Sometimes what is too much for
someone looks small. A mother carries a crying child, an ant
carries a grain of sugar. A child carries love.

Salam.

Every time a chromosome replicates, some genes are lost
at its tail. That's how we age. When I was five, all the boys
in my class were first hooked on sugar, then to *attaboys* from
their dads. Yesterday, when I asked my dad for forgiveness,
I saw an *attaboy* in his hands.

Papa, I am sorry for yesterday.

How do you carry an invisible weight. How do you live standing
on the edge of a blade. God created earth in six days and had to rest on
the seventh. The last time I had a good night's sleep was when my
mother carried me tied to her back.
What else is there to remember.

Allah Hafiz.

A Sickness That Is Absolute

The first time my mother hit my father back, it was Eid; I don't remember
which Eid, the Eid al-Adha or its little sister. It was a long time coming.
We were on our way to our uncle's house. My father was driving while I sat
silently in the back seat of the car, a small hatchback, gray as a dead dove lying
peace-less in a ditch.

Mediating violence came early to me as a child.
"Bas Karo. Stop fighting. Stop hitting each other. Stop. Chacha kya kahe gay
if he finds out (What will Uncle say if he finds out)."
The same *Chacha* whose wife had run after him once at our ancestral
house with a knife as sharp as my mediating skills.
Mediating violence and violence often become interchangeable. No wonder
many presidents offer missiles to mediate peace. Indian men are world famous for
their loyalty. For their faithfulness.
They do everything but run off. That's their métier. They stay.
The first relationship I stayed in lasted seven years. Which is to say, for seven
long years I did everything but leave. I'm always surprised how we become what
we detest. How learning is almost always a passive exercise. What becomes a part
of us is not what we believe but what we see. And I believe we see everything. All
this to say we see only the worst in everything.

When I see a rat, I see a rodent.
When I see a sparrow, I see extinction.
When I see a lion, I see death.
When I see myself, I see a monster.
If I am anything, I am my anxious mother, who, after those little moments of
rebellion, always forgave my dad.
If I am anything, I am my loyal father,
who, with a salivating tongue, always accepted my mother's apologies.
I am an amalgamation.
Of self-hatred and grandiose.
A reversal of everything real,
like a reflection in my full-sized bedroom mirror, right-side left,

forever assimilating violence
after a forever mediating it.

Courage: Making Sure with My Actions That My Mother Knows Her Prayers Don't Work

The first girl whose heart I ever broke
later broke my heart even more.
The world opens up to you in grief, swallows you—
like a paradox. Consider a
blooming rosebud and the universe closing itself into it.
I will always love you, she said the first time we
made love. We shuddered so hard we forgot to
be tender. See? We forgot. ~~Which is to say~~
~~I don't remember what else we forgot.~~ My
grandfather brought home two
wives in his life, my father
one. I have brought none. My mother
thinks my heart is turning into stone,
Find God and you will soften, she says.
Every so often, in the small hours of the night,
half drunk, I find God with someone, and then
I soften. She swallows the moon and moves on.
As a boy I could do no harm,
as a man all I do is harm, *Haram, Haram,*
shouts my father's voice in the middle
of my head, *How will my son face his Lord*, I
see him cry on the *Jai-Namaz*, my mother sitting
beside him, an ocean on her cheek, unsure, should
she pray anymore   or not. See, I am not saying I am
still grieving that first heartbreak. What I am
saying is that I am grieving.

Horrors of My Childhood Horrors

"Paradise lies beneath your mother's feet."
—*Prophet Muhammed*

(I)
One day,
I will avenge
the horrors of my
childhood by kissing
you orange and red, and
all the colors of the sun. In
my city the colors of dawn and dusk
are the same. If a drunk were to wake up
at any one of the two occasions he would have to ask a
passerby for time and for luck. Mother, I am hardly the beginning
of a drunk, still, there is a poem stuck between my teeth, hiding under my
whiskey stench. Mother, I want to be old and unrecognized, not unrecognizable.

(II)
I can
hardly ever
find a face I can see
myself in. Of course *I am beautiful*.
My breath's mutiny is in its refusal to go on,
but I am well tamed and half castrated. You know I love
puppies and become one in my wet dreams. Mother, how come the
prayers have stopped but the begging never does? How come these
beautiful things with halos of God still invite us with their lies, like the
surface of the ocean—so green, sometimes so blue,
why so confusing, Mother, why so full of death?
Just like men who prey upon the innocent
by loving them. Just like you,
Mother. How so like
you.

(III)
Someone
once told me about
the Sahara and the freezing
cold nights of the desert. So, I drank
apricot wine, Mother, I wore a jacket just like
you had taught me, and I went to sleep, only to wake up
drenched, your Qur'anic verses ready at the back of my chest,
and sweat, oh god, so much sweat, flooding out through my clothes to
extinguish this body's fire, do you remember, Mother?
Devil, they say, is enemy of god. Devil, they say, is also
made of fire, Mother, I take up every opportunity
there is to break my own heart. Sometimes
a phone call from you helps, especially
when you narrate prophet's saying
that *God couldn't be everywhere,*
that is why he created moms.
Mother, I used to think
that god lived in my
heart until I fed you
my heart. And of
course like every
one else you
took a bite
and ate
it.

A Bird Flies Not Knowing Why

"Send the beloved child on a journey."
          —*Japanese proverb*

one more day // wasted // away from you,
or maybe one day // closer // to something more.

—

I wanted to tell you what I saw // what made me smile //
but you were gone // far too long // flying high // & I was
too busy // staying put // being invisible.

—

they say every step in the right direction is the destination itself //
          so I am getting a move on.

—

          baby destinations.

—

there is this tender place
between *something & everything*.

now that's where I see myself;

someone's something
in the everything of their world.

—

present // & not vitreous //

not flying // & knowing // exactly why //

human //

—

I need to know which parts of me need to be touched.
there are so many things I do not remember to remember.

Opening

In a town the size of its people,
      I was small. On my back,

I saw, with eyes closed, not
      the woman touching, but her touch.

In my center, a skeleton but boneless,
      attentive to her hands.

She was smiling, which is why
      I cannot forget. Her lips—

I never grew enough to fill.
      Like a toddler, impatient,

unlike my name. Still not asking
      to be spared.

She was smiling with my giggle I remember.
      For in the town the size of its people,

that day, I had grown up. In an instant. Too fast.
      In a moment of feminine virility.

All this to say when one day she stopped,

       I was grown up enough to not be enough—

to go out and find what I had lost.

       To not be spared again

of the touch—of the

       way back, *back*

when I found it all, I would crave

       for the rest of the days.

In Death Everyone Becomes a Buddha

how do you write names in the air. how do you know what you do not know.
how can two apples from the same apple tree taste so different.

one son harvests and reaps the fruit of his work,
      the other witnesses the harvest through the eyes of a scarecrow, smiling.

one listens to love songs,
              the other listens to the silence just after.

one lives in summer-land,
           the other shivers and shivers.

one earns the money,
        the other spends it.

one invents a state and calls it love,
              the other goes out and finds tragedies.

one stares at the TV as it makes faces,
                the other stares at the table and it yawns.

one draws a flower on the canvas,
           the other draws a sneeze.

one is remorseless,
        the other resource-less.

one feels scared,
     the other sad.

one stays because leaving is not an option,
           the other has already left.

Basta

Every so often   I have treated my father like that book I dropped on the dirty
floor   of my middle school classroom   which I was too in a hurry
pre-recess   to pick up   and kiss   and then gently press
against my forehead   asking for forgiveness.

I still remember the school bag I'd put it in every day   a canonical rectangular
bag my father had bought for me: color of the rain   silver buckles and a
few pleated pockets on the front   one plastic handle on top   and two
denim straps on the back to hug my tiny shoulders straight.

It wasn't a school bag to me then   it was my *Basta*   that I carried with me
to and back from school.   I took it with me   when I went to school
every day   when I went for sleepovers at my cousin's house on weekends
when we went on school picnics   when we went on family trips,
always the same kind of heavy but   way too important to leave behind;
it was the way to the future   that my father had thought out for me.

And now   when that future has arrived   see   my father is not
here.   He is still   somewhere   in the past   planning   a still
better future   for that same kid   who still forgets   to pick
him up from the floor and kiss him   and touch him to his forehead   asking
for forgiveness.

Lessons

A rose was born, says my mother,

recalling my birthing,

and I listen intently

all the while thinking

how then

and exactly when did that rose turn

into this homeless weed I see in myself now?

People call me a wildflower man,

a misplaced piece of art,

and believe me I've tried to

place myself there.

In their imagination,

wearing work shirts

and long cotton pants

held together by cufflinks

and leather belts.

Mothers say quite fruitful things if you listen.

"Your balls will stretch to the floor if you

don't wear underpants all hours of the day,"

she had said once, one of those rare times I listened to her in

my preteen years.

I am touching 30 today

and I must say she wasn't wrong at all.

(Well, not touching the floor yet, but it got scary there for a while.)

So now I wear underpants

and let them hold my everything in place most hours of most days

and send prayers my mother's way,

for teaching me such an important lesson.

Some days when I think about the old times,

I wonder if she had been a little less self-involved

and a little more giving,

what other lessons would I have learned?

I wonder if I had been a little less stubborn,

a little less of a post-pubescent ass,

listened to her a little more,

how differently would my life have turned out?

But she was young then, like I am young now,

and I think we should forgive people for when they're young.

Recipe to Lose Your Identity

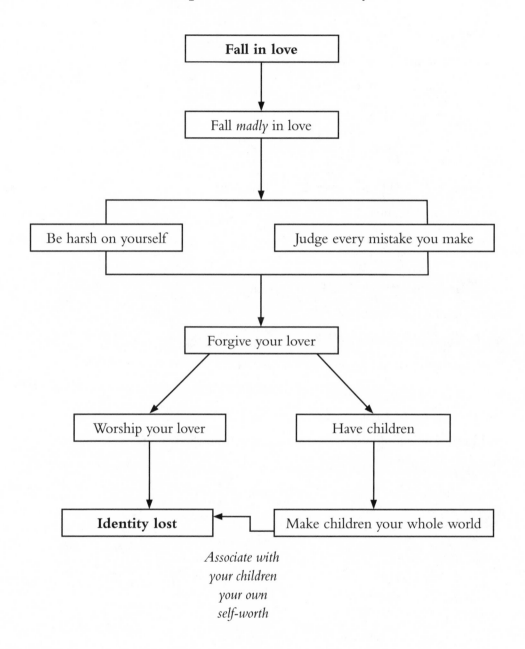

Fall in love

Fall *madly* in love

Be harsh on yourself

Judge every mistake you make

Forgive your lover

Worship your lover

Have children

Identity lost

Make children your whole world

*Associate with
your children
your own
self-worth*

An Autumn Infinite

        youth;   more legend than flesh   i invent then tell
it   lies—truth—lies   again   *youth* a ceremony of rebellion   everything
washed ashore   this sacred commotion i its victim   and you   everyone a
passing leaf   gold   brown   yellow   destined to pass onto
something   something a little darker than sentience   a little less pompous than
life   possibly death   possibly something other than death

               a memory is all i have
               but which one?

        an infant   lost-to-a-car-wreck young-
infant   passed-the-last-smile young infant   juxtaposing itself onto itself   never
to be a teenage boy lost to its *youth*   never a deaf man pretending to hear the
truth   never to kneel down & kiss its own mouth   a caravan of losses but never
a loss   *lies*   half a zero   again   one after the other   penultimate   then
ultimate   *the last breath*   gold   then brown   then yellow   onto something
darker than sentience   a little less pompous than life   possibly death   possibly
something other than death

               a memory is all i have
               but which one?

        a corpse left to this world   an infant   not-yet-
lost-to-a-car-wreck infant   intact   crying itself awake   in another world   a

world away from us   from this   a world not that far   again a *sickness*   a
sickness that lasts forever   *youth*   its name   i its victim   and you   everyone a
passing leaf   an autumn of all four seasons   more legend than flesh   an
invention of a life   a pain that doesn't exist existing   *forever*   lies—truth—
lies   again   rebellion;   *youth*

a memory is all i have
an autumn of all four seasons

an autumn infinite.

Dreamers Dream Dreamers Do

the pillars of creation look like

      the hand of god   and I keep

losing people I love   keep losing people who have loved me

     if I lose gravity, will I fly?   once I jumped through my

         window and landed face-first on the porch   a bird came

      flying to me with a mouthful of worms thinking I were a baby

bird   nursing me loving me   then throwing my

         half-healed body out of the nest again

   flying is hard   you don't just wake up one day and find gravity absent

it takes time   you try to fly   you fall   you get hurt   one thing at a

time you pick your world apart   then get up again   try again   fall

again   sometimes through the hands of people you love   sometimes

        in your own judging eyes   and then all

    of a sudden   the gravity is gone   and you spring up   elevate

      see the world from a distance   know things

     see things   find truths   watch people clearly

as they truly are   in their own loneliness   grappling with their own

dreams   everyone sobbing with the same pain   everyone trying to fly

the same unique flight   everyone locked between the

fingers of the hand of god   alone   losing people they love   still

dreaming big   still hurting   still secretly looking

for open windows to jump from and fly

II

————

WERE WE HOLDING HANDS?

Didicoi / Silent Wayfarer // Habibi /// Night-Eyed Beast

I loved you.
Now I shall mourn.

Always

There are so many dreams sleeping in my eyes

and so many nightmares standing awake and alert.

Every goodbye feels like a beautiful waterfall

crushing the swimmer below it.

Still, I swim. No escape plan in mind.

Even when all I see is you leaving

and it doesn't matter if my eyes are open or closed.

People are always leaving in my eyes.

Riptides of You

Water Flows, Air Flows, Souls Fly, I Fly

& when I am / with you / I become *nabood* / inexistent /

which is to say / I cannot / see / myself anymore /

which is to say / your existence / suffices mine /

I die / I am set free / which is to say /

I don't need / to / *be (mawjud)* anymore /

which is to say /

                 I found you /

which is to say / whatever happens / from now on /

cannot / touch me / cannot / affect me / cannot /

change my fortune: / I have / for once /

flown away / resigned / to wonderland /

to heaven / to you

PLMD

When my legs tired, from all the *walking aways*
I decided to walk *toward* you,
expecting it to cure all the ache.

But our bodies don't work this way.

My leg bones, although healthy,
and covered in an intricate maze of blood lines,
fat blankets, and muscle armor, have found no relief.

Even staying still, this pretending to be content in one place
has only gotten them to move on their own.   My doctor calls
it a disease: "Periodic Limb Movement Disorder,"
PLMD for short, she says.
It is the little sister to Restless Leg Syndrome.

Surprising how the wanderings in our hearts reach these nooks
of our body so slyly,
like a thief stealing rest,
contentment,
joy.
Maybe not joy.   Maybe only joy.

Did you know butcherbirds hunt in packs?
Dolphins masturbate
Monkeys whore around

Snakes, although famous for their bite, don't chew their prey,   only swallow.

My chest sucks air in   even when it's the last thing I want it to do.
My heart beats itself to no death   every second of every day   when all I
need is   some rest.
My legs walk me to people I don't want   to love.
My body,   a slave to something outside me,

      I embody cravings I don't know how to name

      I weep oceans when no one sees me

      Even when the alarm clock goes off

      This nightmare doesn't break.

The Snapshot of a Scientist Frozen in Time

I.

When you left, I became terrific

for a couple of hours, maybe a week.

I think it was your absence

and your warmth from years of presence.

Multitude of factors

home science

chemistry

geography

biology

that sparked this change.

II.

Everything deteriorated a few days later.

I read laws of thermodynamics to understand how

heat dissipated so quickly once people left.

I found no answers.

I read histories of world wars to understand how egos fell

when heroes were doomed for failure.

I became an addict.

To substance.

Just to understand my cravings.

III.

My substances soon poured into poems,

which leads me to this.

This moment

where on a cold summer's night

I am writing in agony.

Still trying to understand how everyone has

done this before.

And how everyone will do it again.

Even us.

Even us.

Platanus × acerifolia

Approximately
15.3% of trees in New York
are London plane trees / and a little
Google search also tells me that they are the world's most
reliable city trees / 27% of trees in Connecticut are red maple trees /
So when I lived in Connecticut it made me extremely lucky to
have a London plane tree grow just outside the window of my sleeping room.
Every autumn I'd wait for its leaves to fall off / & as the full moon rose every two weeks
& then / began its setting / post midnight / I could see the shadows from the tree's
naked branches / like arms / travel toward me / deliberately / first at the windowsill /
then at the foot of my bed / then over my sheets / closing in
on my neck / never long enough to touch where it'd count / but enough to play / frisk.
I think the moon rose to the highest of its heights and then fell to its daily deaths
just to tease me / every fortnight / to give me a taste of what might be.
It knew
all my fetishes /
all my sadistic appetites /
and like all of nature:
callous / foxy /
it knew
if it held back
long enough
it'd deprive me enough to seduce me.

Until Then Love Me Like This

You don't like how the nature sounds   so you close your windows
you roll down the curtains   I think you can also love me like this:
without light   without sound   like a duty / a meal / a destiny
like a hangman and his rope / a bullfrog and its prey / a prophet and the dead.
Even a lobster has a falling out with its own shell about twenty-five times in the
first five years of its life   that's part of its growth   how
preposterous to think we can touch heights without stretching our arms out
without kicking and stomping the past?   I have been told plucking stars
out of the night sky is not considered stealing   but I like to think
otherwise   I prefer to leave the stars where they are and mind my own
business   I break lines in my poems instead like I used to break bones
in car wrecks   I break hopes of a hope in people's eyes instead like
alcoholics break crystal glasses in all-you-can-drink bars: swiftly   and
without thought   loudly   and without exception.
They say what feels like poison is often poison   what feels like balm is often
balm   that life's meaning rests in the hands of gods bigger than our
demons   so I dream in auguries to console myself: *what is bound to*
happen will happen   what was deemed to be will be   once
I am reshaped in the shape of you   slowly   over time   like a
stone chiseled at the riverbed   I will find foreheads to crack   I will
find eye sockets to strike   I will cut my flesh into pieces and have these
pieces thrown off a cliff   like confetti   a miscellany of loss   which is
to say I will go looking for my celebration   which is to say I will fly away
from this   which is to say I will crash some other place I don't belong
which is to say until then can you keep loving me this bitter love   keep

bruising my frightened ego with your welcoming teeth   until the end
is nearer than the start will you keep handing me box after box of affection with
its assortment of all kinds of defeat?   You see it is only a matter of time I look
in   the   mirror   and   see   nothing.

Stuck in a Melancholy Flower

What meaning to find in this life so permanently without you?

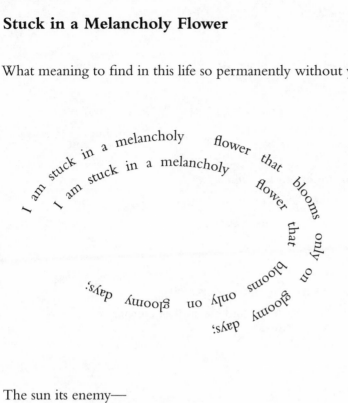

The sun its enemy—
      I am forced to hide;

      you see,
      lonely people smile   in the **center**   of their

                    l o n e l i n e s s.

This is not to make amends (*understand the distinction*)
but to crack open their mouths.   To let the air in.
To understand the last of their *sanity*
and the firsts of the *insanity* of this world.

I am   a mirror image   of *one* of   my
future selves;
       A reflection | noidɔɘ⅃ɟɘɿ A
     of a dingy old man | nɒm blo ʏgnib ɒ ʇo

               Separated from love *inside love*
                   laughter *inside laughter*,
                      joy *inside joy*,

           stuck
                for an eternity
                and eternity of eternities.

Palliative Care

"Row, row, row your boat, gently down the stream.
Merrily, merrily, merrily, merrily, life is but a dream."
—*Nursery rhyme*

We fucked on her father's funeral   not because we were horny little
teenagers   rather because we didn't know what else to do   but you
know we were young   natural predators   endings were not final   wasted
so much   time   hurt   nothing fatal   we burned   each
other   smoked our eyes   did it so much   we vanished   from our own
vision   imbibed lust out from each other
yearned

<u>called it   love</u>

<u>called it love</u>

<u>called it</u>   **love**

<u>called it</u>

<u>love</u>

now we are older   grayer
perspicacious

we have kissed mouths we didn't think kissable   we have touched people
we still   cannot   touch   we still   touch   suckle sin out from
their fingers

<u>still call it love</u>

<u>still call it</u>

love   <u>still call it</u>

<u>love</u>

<u>still</u>

Post-Laughter Guilt

am i without a lover when you look
the other way;
am i alive when you're asleep?

the first time a magician showed me a magic trick
i felt weak at my knees,
the last time i saw you walk away,
all i felt was small.

what kind of vanity is this,
what egotism?
the ones forgotten are forgotten but that *one* forgotten always becomes a poem.

of course, sitting in this world, i am far away from this world.
amounts to nothing, does it?

you are not here
and i am still breathing do you hear me?

last night i laughed so hard i cried do you understand?
everything was so clear nothing made sense at all.

and today,
all this post-laughter guilt

and
thinking about sitting in the
pouring rain beside you &
f a l l i n g   a p a r t.

i a m
s till
f alling
a p art.   i s till f eel s o s mall.
going in circles, still learning to let you go.

Elegy ~~for Our Unborn Child~~ – 1   & 2

"The best and the worst thing about winters is their going away. People share the same habit, and this breaks everyone's heart."

(I)

When you left, all the departures stopped, do you understand?
Years passed but nothing left, do you understand?

> I am everything without you but myself
> (am I *somewhere?*)

(II)

How do you put life in the hands of death,
day after day, year after year, and not grieve?

I have grieved like a shy poplar—
stood my ground without making a sound.
But silence grows on you like debt,   like the shadow of that monster beside
> your childless childhood bed
> (am I *someone?*)

(III)

They say, often a childless father himself becomes the child
(maybe an attempt to mitigate the distance.)

They say, unborn children are sent to heaven
but what about those left behind who live in sadness?
What heaven is there for us?

> (I am *something*
> running to and from
> *somewhere* and *someone,*
> *someone* and *somewhere,*
> *somewhere* and *someone x 5*)

> Where are you?

Anomaly

When she says *you're special*, all I hear is
you're an anomaly.
When she says *I love you*, all I hear is the *I*.

I am not saying I am any different from
a lot of them, but when you have seen people
run away all your life, you understand
the point of staying more than anything else.

However, this in no way means that when it's
your time to stay, you necessarily do.

Gateless Home

If there were a place as lonely as two people deeply in love,
it must be this,
where *I love you*'s hit you and fall right off, one after the
other, and not one ever pierces your carapace and lodges into your soul.
"How do you build homes out of defeat?" asks my intrepid heart.
"You don't," I throw my answer back. *"You live out on the
streets, with other lonely folks, or you spit spiderwebs and reside in
them hoping for someone to walk through and get caught up in
your gateless home."*

Meditations

(every day brings a memory   every memory a smile   a joyful tear   a
meaningful moment   a meditation.)

were you in your *burqa*   was it a *naqaab*   did it hide you well   were you
safe   do you not like these questions   is it strange that i left out all the
question marks   do i know you too well   do i still cry for you   why
do i ask questions for the both of us   why don't i have the answers   were
you gone before i was   did i leave without a pause   were our destinations
different   was my *burqa* a horrible color   were we looking for
something better   did we find it   did we take off our *naqaab*   did the
mirror hold our image in its palm   did it remind us of our past   did we want
to go back   did we find what we were looking for   did we find each
other all over again   did we have the courage to stay   did we die a happy
death   were we holding hands?

The Absence of Everything

(Not All Flowers Are Beautiful, Not All Solitude Becomes a Sanctuary)

How do you forget something that's unforgettable?
Something that lives on the surface of your being.

Something that makes you so naked you turn inside out.
Once I was in love and it was magnificent;

I became the glorified version of myself and it
was no fluke. I raised the tides of the sea on command in my dreams

and she praised me for it. The dreams never went away, they still don't,
and in my dreams she weeps for me, like an infant.

We were never blessed with a child
so one day I decided to become one. Threw my body in her lap and cooed myself to sleep.

When we buried our first stillborn, he looked like soft flesh.
Still as new as in his mother's womb. We didn't know it back then,

but we had wrapped him with our souls before lowering them into the opened ground.
It has been years now and I still don't know what symbolism to make out of

all the flowers that blossom on our child's grave. What blessings
to infer out of this mockery that Mother Nature makes of us. Bringing us gift after gift of

grief and then laughing in our faces with color and scent.
His mother, now a mother with someone else, sometimes I think of her

and wonder how she must feel holding a healthy child in her arms.
How she conceived something so alive with someone else.

And I miss them, still. I miss them so much that I play hide-and-seek with my own reflection. Hardly anyone ever comes to find me when the countdown ends, and I don't know

if I should like this loneliness or weep. I don't know if I should move on with my life as well, or simply coo myself back to sleep.

For Madness

I will burn like a candle   slow, and through the night   this is another one
of those full-mooned nights that movies had us believe belonged to the
wolves   I hear crickets chirp instead I have said this before   do wolves
chirp when they feel sad?   you see, psychology tells me I regress in times of
stress   whimper like a pup hit by a car   roll up on my bed into a cotton
ball   p(r)ocessed and petal-soft   *chirp chirp chirp*   once a
woman touched me and I almost vanished   like sterile water—evaporated
into an eternity   and then left   I don't know if I ever came back from
that   or if I ever will   this goer   this sinner   this doer of
wrong   I don't know what sorcery   what crystal ball what divination to
assimilate   to return to where I was   girlchild-innocent baby-
new   pollen-fresh   elastic   ordinary   these days cold touches me
and I condense   roll down my own cheek and **fall**   *chirp*
chirp   *whimper whimper*   my psychiatrist tells me, *everything is cold*
when you can't feel the warmth. I believe him, then condense and **f**

a

l

—

The girl on the train tells me,   *everything is warm when you yourself are the*
source of the warmth   I believe her too, again condense and **f**

a

l

—

A long time back Rumi said something that stayed with me   or should I
say that I stayed with   *let yourself be silently drawn by the stronger pull*
of what you really love, he said   hence began this experiment   of letting
myself get pulled a little every day into the abyss of my inherent madness   of
allowing myself to go to grounds no one dares set foot on

                    hoping
                    someday
                    someone
                    in some ugly corner of the world

                    awaits
                    to know me
                    to touch me
          and turn me back into my conventional self again

Until then,
                    I surrender
                    to lunacy
                    to folly
                    to madness
                    to myself.

The Lover Disappears & the Mirror Falls Silent

"In relationships with others . . . the other is nothing but a mirror."
        —Osho

lover — the world hasn't been kind — the days have gotten darker — the music has turned to noise — sex has become a chore — life has started to taste bitter — although I'm still fastened to the last time I saw you smile — I have come to understand sad people smile — a lot — you always smiled — a lot —

        I know you are gone — I also know you were never here — do you know that I still speak to your memory — that's how I dilute the bitterness on my tongue — I have heard that practice makes perfect — lover — why am I perfect only when I am absent?

        today if you asked me why I did what I did I would tell you the truth — lover — please don't ask me why I did what I did because I will tell you the truth.

        I am going to keep writing to you — about you — about us — till the end of time — or — until I convince myself that we happened — that you were here — with me — near me — in me —

        lover — we happened —
        and a hell of a lot happened to us —

what if we happened in each other's blind spots —
what if we ruined everything we built together —
shattered our very own homes —
emptied out each other —

everyone around is ruining their own life —
everyone around is living in their own blind spot —
completely hollowed out —

        how many times should we martyr ourselves and our
own innocence in the name of growing? — in the hope of becoming someone
better?

        lover — I know you lived — you smiled —
        you happened — we happened —

        and everyone should know too —

        lover — tell them —
            one last time — tell them.

Some Questions from a Past Self to the Present Self

Have you been stranded in the middle,
on your knees, as if begging (for the right to stay)?
Have you been lost, and if you have been lost,
have you been found?
What is this one urge that keeps you up at night?
And do you like it when you are up so late?
What makes the hair on the back of your neck stand?
And when it stands, do you think it needs a reason?
Do you think you have it in you to say something good in words?
And if you do, do you think you would ever say them out loud?
Are your lungs full?
(Full of shame, full of guilt, full of hope.)
Have you found life in your dark room,
or have you discovered some secret glee, some
schadenfreude in all this pain?
Do you ever wish to get out?
And will your choice change if you know I am standing outside?
What if I am standing outside and waiting?
What if I am standing outside and not?

———————

Alternative title(s) for this poem:

Exercise: Replace the **title** of the above poem with this
Some Questions For [Insert Name★]
and read the poem again.

★The name can be anyone's (except your own).

This Is How I Still Keep Holding On to You

(Part I)

I keep holding on to you by doing things I never got to do with you.

(Simple things. Like sitting quietly at the beach.)

And I obsess. God, do I obsess!

I compulsively misspell your name in my journal:

I have had this thought for years now,

that if I got your name right, in writing, even if just once,

all my wrongs might vanish.

(I need to remember the wrongs I did to you.)

No, I don't love you anymore. Time heals everything but not without a cost.

(It consumes our medicine to do its job.)

A friend once told me a story of his youth. Of a time, when forced away from his

lover

he resorted to writing in a notebook, hourly, the number

of hours he was stuck there, away from her.

He insisted there were 2183 hours in total for that summer.

It's heaven only, he said, when it is over.

(I couldn't gather the courage to ask him when what is over? The hours of separation or the

love in our heart?)

No, I don't love you anymore.

Maybe this is just my way of making my life feel *in progress*;

moving ahead and not in moribund stagnation.

(It's amusing how we don't have to lift a finger to get closer to death. It just comes on its

own.)

Moribund: Such a misleading word. Where you don't move toward
the end but the end itself travels to you.
(Whatever it might seem, the journey belongs to death and nothing more.)

(Part II)

Someone once said,

there is no greater anguish than to recall a happy time when miserable.

I remember how I felt love in my heart, every minute of every day,

the turquoise blue eyes of my youth, so transparent.

(All see-through things belong to heaven. Nothing youthful is worthy of wrong.)

I don't know who divided time into hours, minutes, and seconds.

But I think there is time between time. There are seconds between seconds.

Minutes between minutes. Hours between hours — *the side effects of missing you.*

Once my physics teacher told me that it took thousands of years for

the light of some stars to reach us, and by the time we experienced that light,

there's a high chance that star's long gone. Passed on.

(I wanted to tell you that your light finally reached me. It took its time but it's here. It's

important that you know.)

I don't tell anyone about my day. No matter how big or small, whatever happens lies buried in my heart.

(Yes, this is how I keep holding on to you.)

But no, I don't love you anymore.

Love is the incomprehensible longing for something we want.

The knowledge that there is a final piece out there

that will complete our soul's eternal halves. And god, do I keep looking!

(I hope you keep looking too.)

Promise

I don't know when I became
a half of everything I
used to be.

Half weed
half flower.

Half strength
half coward.

Half life
half death.

Half earth
half gravel.

This is my SOS call
with no device to press the
buttons on.

Can you come and save me?
I will rip you to pieces
and eat you whole, I promise.

Will you come?

Restricted Entry

If   .again open will you to door this and break might curse

I		this
ration		how
all		that's
that		Maybe
I		forgiveness.
have,		their
save		me
every		grant
little		and
bit		me
of		of
joy		remember
I		will
feel,		wronged
forgive	(only	have
myself	happy	I
for	people	someone
everything	may	maybe
I	enter)	memory,
did,		their
I		of
do,		worthy
I		me
still		find
do,		will
I		wronged
won't		have
do,		I
if		someone
I		maybe

accordion all that I have ever felt, club together enough strength,

Calling a Mountain a Spade

All that scares me makes me lighter.
Will you float away with me? To a

town where the sun's slow exile doesn't
threaten our days. Where the counting of

hours is simply an exercise in futility.
Where wasting away years is the norm of

the place. Someplace where I mother you,
and you can mother me. Without resistance.

Without practice. Like children playing House
and winning. Like Mute Swans restoring their

nest from last year and starting a new family.
Where we can be siblings and offspring, lovers

and mystics, and anything. *Anything. Does what
scares you make you lighter as well?*

Don't answer. We can still play pretend.
We can still play pretend.

sometimes what we call love can be an ugly thing

sometimes i stand in the white gaze of snow
the sun beating its anger-laced love all over it;
a cigarette in one hand and your memory in the other
thinking about how you might be holding his child
this very moment
pulling it to your breast, handing it the warm presence of life,

and how on these dull winter afternoons he would
come back tired from work
and look at your face to feel something.
each day the same routine;
the child growing feathers with each rental breath
your eyes full of motherly grace, and him finding something
new in you to love every single day.

you saved so much inside you I never knew one could hold;
a heart so full of benevolence god had to birth people like me for equilibrium.

they say entropy is the measurement of disorder within a system;
the arrow of time that turns everything to a mess. the inherent tendency of
matter to gravitate toward a state of maximum chaos.

sometimes i think entropy is simply love trying to kill us.
and i am sorry i died.
i am sorry you had to fall in love again.

Notes on Rakeeb without *Qaafiya*

He errs, he makes mistakes, but he makes amends
every single time, doesn't he?
Talks without pretense, listens without judgments, doesn't he?

Once old, love, like plastic bags in the sea, doesn't rot but
kills all life around;
He tells you love doesn't work like this at all, doesn't he?

Transparent heart, your bedside doll, your knight in lustrous silver,
diamonds, and gold;
He says "sorry" and means it, cares for *my* sickling, doesn't he?

He doesn't make you feel what you don't want to feel, follows
a pleasant routine;
Counts mermaids for you when you can't fall asleep, doesn't he?

Sometimes, the timing can be wrong, but if you just stay strong,
the right time will come;
He tells you leaving's not an option, doesn't he?

Kisses recklessness out of your needs, melts your heartache in
the sheets, says goodnight
Every night; he thinks this is your vision for a life, doesn't he?

It has been a year since you two met, you will tell me the
story when it ends,
He promises forever of forevers, doesn't he?

In sickness and in health, he doesn't run off like Akif does,
he catches you when
You fall, but lets you forge your smiles from afar, doesn't he?

—*He still holds you when you cry, doesn't he?*

The Boy & The Wolf

1.

i am standing
in front of me
a wolf

baby-eyed
skin-soft fur
but so very hard to love

the wolf the boy doesn't cry of
the ripples in the river punch and
distort its face

2.

a wolf standing
in front of me
a boy

clumsy-wonder
man-child plump
one who needs to be loved

the boy the wolf didn't consume
cries to the world, cries to
a different shame

3.

there is a different truth   they've hidden from the world
a different lie that they have told

4.

the wolf the boy doesn't cry of   &   the boy the wolf didn't eat
they both share a name

5.

the wolf the boy doesn't cry of   &   the boy the wolf didn't eat
both in fact are one and the same

Falling into Love / Neither Here nor There

I was born with a tongue but tongueless   with big round cheeks but

smileless   feistily looking around trying to find old things new to me

chewing on them   toothless   this is my story of finding a taste for

the world   this is how I knew how to pace myself into a familiarity

which I would hide under my armpit for years to come   bear with me

I grew up like grass   swiftly and sharp   into a wonderful little boy

bred an exquisite mustache the size of my world   until one day

when my uncle held me by the chin and shaved it away   and

everyone knows   when boys shave their mustaches they fall into love

a love where they lose everything under their armpits to the universe of

endless summers   a love away from anything they understand   make

mistakes to learn new lessons   kill lovers to find new killers   isn't

nature weird this way?   a lion falls in love with a motionless gazelle

a vulture with rotting meat   means nothing to you does it?   see,

I don't know whether I am the lion or the gazelle   the vulture or

the rotting meat   but I am still here am I not?   still just a boy

I will learn these things when I fall into love again

III

———

HITCHED TO NOTHING

Dreamer of Utopia / Raven-Haired Child

Against Madness

sometimes I try to recognize parts of me unmolested by time   and I
swear to God all I recognize is a forgotten part of me filled with zeal   this
fullness   consider a new mother's breasts   ready to nurture what life's come
before her   not knowing how much enough is enough   not knowing when
to stop the feeding   they say I'm meant to be of use to this
world   but I flood everything I cross   disturb the harmony of all
the nature's songs   dangle from both ends of all strings   pushing and
pulling   trying my hardest to stay still   some days I am a father to my
father   some days again I am his disheveled son   round and
round   life misbehaves with me every time I try to kiss it on the
mouth   so I lock myself up   in my darkness   in my temporary
asylum   away from all the horrors of the world   and then   like some
sick joke   the sun with all its hunger finds a crevice and creeps in   to wake
me up and push me out again   makes me wonder if in some past life I
lived as a mongoose who died from the bite of its half-eaten snake   a severed
venomous head still dangling from my rib   a heart marred
enough   eyes contaminated enough with some poison that makes you
look at this world through the tainted glass of a past death   a death I do not
remember   once I saw a struggling rabbit being eaten by a dog   it made
me so greedy I became the dog   fantasized about the taste of life on my sour
tongue   once deep in the forest I took a breath so full I had to be
locked away in a psychiatric ward   this world is such a terrifying
place   but   so soft under my skin   so clean I wanted to gouge it out
and gift it back to God

Sometimes Loss Looks Like a Mirror

Like there is nothing that can wet the sky / there is nothing that our eyes won't see. /
I am at a loss when I look at the mirror / which itself looks like loss. / Last night, a lover said,

Sky is a mirage. /	*To which I said, /*
This smile is a	*mirage, / this*
body is a secret	*debt; / A pact*
between a mur-	*-derer and a saint. /*
Last night / I	unhooked the
covers off her	breasts / whispered
every forgetta–	–ble sentence a lover
has ever said /	the sound of my name
crescendoed /	like sinister music /
through the night;	the same two syllables
slapping the four	walls of her room /
like some kind	of punishment for bad
taste / over &	over / over & over
again / making	then unmaking
ourselves / two	bodies committed /
like suicidal child–	–ren to asylums / like
juvenile delin–	–quents to jails / lost /
burrowing caves	to heaven / spelunking
through blood /	away from their
demons / away	from their shames /
& this question	condensed like an

ocean in a raindrop / this question / unasked / unanswerable; / how can we find ourselves
inside each other when all of us have already run away from ourselves. A long long time ago.

What is fair. What has been fair. What would be fair. Why fair. Who promised it?

What is fair?

The past throws me into the future every time I try to visit an old friend.
The future wants me to stay put.
So what do I do? I stay put. In the present. Like an old out-of-work pendulum.
Like unreclaimable snakeskin buried under the desert sand.
Do we rename a *football* to *Mr. Sphere* when it is discarded in the landfill? Does this *Mr. Sphere* like it when no one kicks him around anymore?
Is music still music when the notes are played in a vacuum? Is love still love when the person you love is gone?

What has been fair?

Option-less, I am a man of the moment. Made by everything and anything.
I stare at the fake stars on my room's ceiling but don't wish upon the dead light.
I have nothing left to ask for. *Answer these questions:* Does a lonely scorpion sting itself? Does an angry lion eat its own tongue? Does a leafless poplar stand in shame? Does art beg for admiration?
Shut up.

What would be fair?

A tigress doesn't eat her prey out of spite. She eats it to satisfy her appetite. So what if I have lost all my appetite. For life. I am still living. Breathing. Asking questions. I am still as alive as anyone else. Still as lost as any other guy. What if I eat a little too much, sleep a little too long, cry a little too hard, love a little too small; I am still here. I am still here, living this life as unfairly as I can. Stuffing my body with sugar, turning my blood to sap, regurgitating words I must have imbibed from my mother's lap. *Apple. Pomegranate. Carrot juice. Lime. Chicken wings. Wine. Wine. Whine.*

Why fair?

Do the stars know that they shine? Does the rose care when it is plucked? Are penguins repulsed by warmth? Once I heard of an old man who died in his sleep the very morning his grandson was born. Once my father told me about the hardships that led him to God. One night I got so high I became God's masturbating arm. The first time I was molested, it was September. It was beautiful. I don't remember the rest.

Who promised it?
Liars.

Who promised it?
Shut up.

Who promised it?
Everyone.

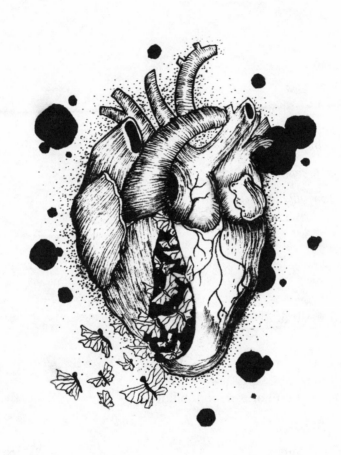

Simple

i

"who said the life of a toddler was a metaphor for carefree?

as a toddler, i was a burning house of caution,

tiptoeing my way to my teens

now look at me,

after a lifelong battle,

fight after fight

to abandon this caution,

i am burned down to cinders

i suppose this is how childhood sets me free."

i

my contempt is

always one step ahead of

my maturity:

this growing up to phosphorus responsibilities

merrily blazing away

all my breathable dreams

makes me wonder,

when Surdas said

that he saw God naked (*"Dekhe ri Hari nangam nanga"*)

did he actually mean that
he saw the truth?

when Khusrow said
that he was an infidel-of-love (*"Kafir-e-ishqam"*)
did he actually mean
that he believed in love
and nothing else?

my metaphors are simple
but i worry how hard it
will be for them to understand
that when i say *i see God crying*
what i mean is that i see my soul
still stuck in childhood wonder

when i say *i am not myself anymore*
what i mean is that i am
still someone i was once

i
we learned about mitosis in seventh grade in great detail
but now when i think of mitosis i think
of the heart growing *full* and then
breaking into *two*

of course, there is no rejecting the existence of pain,
no rejecting the existence of love

so when i say *God is a feeling inside this ache*
what i mean is that he is more ache, he is more
of this breaking, he is more of us getting full and
maybe not dividing but instead wanting
to be *two.*

i

you know why a toddler doesn't mind dying?

because a toddler no matter how cautious
doesn't mind living.
and this, this is what imprisons me.

So Much More

"It's rather the exhaustion from life that people often mistake for our fascination with death."

What if

all these stories died / unsaid / unwritten/ unexplained / like mysteries /
in search of worthy ears / calamities / looking furiously for cheers / to seize / to
snatch /

Question: who is deserving of what? / *Question:* is bereavement an active
exercise / *or* / do we mourn everything / everybody / every day / every moment /
every breath? / isn't grieving an out-of-form repentance / a delayed actualization
of remorse / but remorse is always badly timed so i believe what we lose is what
we lost a long time ago / *flying shampoo bubbles / fallen rose petals / this little
angel /*

i believe what we gain is already gained at a loss / *birthing of her wonderful
baby brother / his quirky sense of humor / his fascination with death / his death /
his funeral* / all a downhill illusion of an exercise / like pedaling a bicycle with no
real need of pedaling / a life unworthy

of anything? / his face pale as if burdened
with foresight / his hands fiercely tender in an afterlife / his feet finally without
holes / without the running / his skin as taut as the precise moment of his leaving /
his mind / finally learned enough to omit the omissions / finally calm / finally
perfect / his existence (or lack thereof) / finally uneventful and boring like he
always prayed for his life to be / like his sister still does / that little angel / still
frozen / lost / in flying shampoo bubbles / decaying slowly from outside inward /
mourning his death

and so much more

There is a girl who likes fire

and she asks me with a confident face,

"we will work, right?"

and of course i lie to her

and tell her he is in it for the long haul.

all this while he sits looking at

me as if he believes me.

that's how it goes.

people in love don't doubt love,

yet it always goes to shit.

always the same story:

one person falls in love

until the other person falls in love even more,

and that's how the fall is broken.

abruptly.

always with this sudden jerk

shoving us back into reality.

all bones intact,

but the hearts, O the hearts,

always in pieces,

never to be the same again.

A Juneberry Plant Doesn't Blossom in June

"मेरे लफ़्ज़ों की गहराई मेरी बीमारी नहीं
क्या मेरी बीमारी मेरे लफ़्ज़ों की गहराई है?"

میرے الفاظ کی گہرائی میری بیماری نہیں
کیا میری بیماری میرے الفاظ کی گہرائی ہے؟

i

a juneberry plant doesn't blossom in june
a moth disguised as a wasp cannot sting
a person in deep sleep is not dead
my depression is not meaningful.

it is not.
it does not give my words any depth.

i

i self-diagnose myself with all the sicknesses of the world   the doctor
confers   calls me a hypochondriac   yet i am not afraid of the germs   it is some
hell of a craving   an insane loneliness in the sponge of my bones   where i
want to culture the darkness of this world   where i want to give bacteria a safe
home

                                                    but when you yourself live in a
halfway house   how do you afford the luxury to nurture?   how do you will
into existence some maniacal dream of living with disease and still being disease
free

i

my depression doesn't give my words depth   but it does provide me
enough silence to drown my wisdom   it does give me solitude where i can be
one with myself and my sickness   something i have learned from people in fair
health

                                        but like everyone ordinary   i don't
find comfort in the diagnoses   it simply makes me crave more illness   more
disease

i

you know how empathy degrades you?
it pays for peace with war   for words with disease   me and my disease
always in a lover's spat   fighting and then shaking hands just to be lovers again

like clockwork i refuse to speak to my sickness   then my sickness refuses to let
me speak with the world   and we are united again   always together
always one   always lonely   always an anguished child in the mirror
always ready   always a bastard smile plastered on his face   always lying
always burning   his future behind him   always trying his best to get a move
on

Hitched to Nothing

"tera tuj ko saomp dey   kya lagat hai mor?   mera muj mein
kuch na hi   jo hovat so tor"   (Let me give you all that is yours.
What worth am I? In me nothing is mine, whatever is, it's yours.)
            —*Amjad Islam Amjad*

            Of course the soul is naked and free.
            and so will you be.   like god.
            like magic.   like rain.   like love.
            like defeat.
Once i heard a man sing   and for the first time i felt the hair on the back of my
neck rise.   in grace.   in absolution.   in honor.   in reverence.   he
sang of a certain someone he'd accepted as god,   and how he didn't need permission
from anyone anymore   not even from that god   to prostrate for that certain
someone.

            Flowered on fire   free
            some pure kind of magic
            he kept singing;

            flooding and flushing,   for
            something as simple as *one-sided love*;
      for something as pious as *the best kind of defeat.*

He kept going on and on   like a mystic hitched to nothing.
And like a madman lost in reverie   i heard him win.

The Voyager

Nietzsche saw an overworked horse being flogged in the middle of the
road and collapsed holding it

                    van Gogh cut his own ear for god knows what,
and confided in Frédéric Salles a request to be confined to an
asylum

                    the first eternity I fell for was a girl in my class

the last lover I mourned hadn't left yet   in fact we were *madly* in love
                      means nothing to you, does it?
I don't know what it is we lose when we lose our minds   sometimes
I touch a man and forget my breath   sometimes a blade touches
me and nothing happens

                                  it has been
late September in my life all my waking hours   the old pomegranate
tree in the yard has never blossomed   the birches in my way have always
been naked   the voyager on my shattered ship always rid of a life
jacket   once in the hospital I witnessed a boy who didn't understand
death die of cancer

                   will you laugh with me at nature's sleight of hand
God doesn't make mistakes   *God doesn't make mistakes*   *God*
doesn't   *doesn't God?*
          ages ago I blazed away all my wonder   a moment later
I started praying for more   according to everyone I self-destruct
according to laws of nature I should be dead   but look at me   this
watering mouth   these trembling hands   this translucent body
healthy as a farm pig   looking for something no one has heard of
still here   still here   mindless   unfazed   living this punishment.

Episode I—*Clinical* Depression

"Oh, monsters are scared," said Lettie. "That's why they're monsters."
—*Neil Gaiman*

A barking dog seldom bites / A crying infant often latches onto
any nipple-shaped thing. / When I was little, I barked and chewed on rubber teats.
/ Watered my feet. / Sprouted. / Found the sun. / Spoke to God as if he were a
friend. /

Is this it? //

A muted life is springing out of my depression. / The unwashed dishes on
the side of my bed are festering maggots, / maggots are
turning magically to flies, / flies are flying with zeal to nowhere / like me /
completing this messed up *circle of life.* //
Maybe there is a monster in all this / and ~~it's me~~ *it's this disease.*

SUICIDE

risk factors
(mnemonic: SAD PERSONS)

Sex - male
- females attempt more, males succeed more

between

Age - >45 years

sincere pity

Depression or other mental illness

and

Previous suicide attempt

insincere kindness

Ethanol/substance abuse

of the world

Rational thoughts/Race
- whites at higher risk

the routine of life

Sickness - chronic illness

turns stale

Organized plan/access to weapons

& the mallard at the lake

No spouse
- marriage is protective
- children of divorced parents at risk

stops singing its song

Social support lacking/Socioeconomic class
- upper-class professionals at increased risk

& flies away.

I Am God I Am Not

as I tend to my wounds,
and hide from my yesteryears,
I am thrown into *the future*
or into *a future* some absent god
keeps writing for me.

there is this strict rule the universe runs by:
all destinies must be preserved.
except when said god changes his mind
and wants to play sick games.

today, when I speak, I might break a very old silence

yes,   I   can be god,
                 can play god,
                 am god,

                 I am god

                 but

if there is a dreamer sleeping somewhere
wearing rags and newspapers to keep warm,
I am not god.

if there is a woman somewhere getting all beat up by a man she has loved,
I am not god.

if there is a child somewhere doubting his existence, or dying
of a famine or a missile,
I am not god.

if there are dimwits elected as prime ministers or presidents,
I am not god.

I am not god when it's all cheesecakes and summertime,

I am not god when it's all vintage smiles and butterflies,

I am not god when I do what I set out to do,

I am not god when I make everyone proud,

but

in my mistakes, I am god.

in my resistance, I am god.

in my fuck-you letters to god, I am god.

Is there a place where regret comes from?

(I)

I am terrified of the center of my heart;
it is diseased with life,
it suffers want.

(II)

Once it made me rip the flesh on my body open
to see if Christmas lights flashed inside of me.

To its surprise everything was unbelievably dark
and extravagantly red
and incredibly painful.

(III)

Salt sprinkled out of my eyes.   I felt so sorry for the friends of my spleen.

(IV)

There is a punishment for every thing in life
and I have done every thing there is to do:
I have loved mermaids dizzy in the red sea.
I have snuck into clouds for free drinks.
I have poured searing wax over lovers I *almost* loved,
and who *almost* loved me.

(V)

I have already kissed my father a thousand stunning goodbyes.

(VI)

Now it feels like I will be spending the rest of my
life writing suicide notes and apologies.
Now it feels like no matter how many nights I spend turning them off,
each morning god's going to turn the lights back on for me.

(VII)

Even though a long time ago, it all ended, still,
there is never going to be an end to me.

A World Where Everything Ceases to Conceal Us; A Quandary

as i age
everywhere around me
the boys are turning into their fathers
the girls into their mothers
as if the universe has nothing new to offer.
        so i hide.

      i close my eyes.

there never has been a future in my eyes.
you see, i am to disappear
            before the future arrives.

but nothing ever happens here
everything just grows
people just change
morph into their monsters.

i am not to open my eyes and see anything other than what is already in me.
i have seen enough.
i cannot both survive this world and be in this world.

i am not a butterfly, only its child. only its child.

I Find God Everywhere There Is Nowhere to Go

I have been thinking of love in abstractions.

is not wanting your father to leave *love*?
is not letting your child suffer *love*?
does love mutate in form,
                   like cancer, like evening skies, like last names, like octopodes?

when I was a child I loved music as much as I loved my father
and for that my mother sits jealous to this day.

the prophet said, "when *love* is for the sake of Allah, it never dies."
and then Nietzsche said, "God is dead."

this is life,
                 we are trained to be house cats, die like house cats,
                 then rise on doomsday, so we rise,
                 today, tomorrow, and God holds our hand everywhere he is present
                 but far from saving anything.

you see *love* in abstract form is   *nothing*
and I don't know how many more times prophets have
to come back and tell us, God, our God, their God, by God,
He *loves* everything.

I Love You

whenever I talk about love, I talk of it in the past

and whenever I talk about death, I talk of it in the future,

as if there is no space for present in my thoughts, as if, for me,

the present doesn't exist.

but just because I am writing in this time, this present,

it must exist, must it not?

dear sir, you are not dead. you are as much alive as the

next person.

dear sir, you will fall in love again, hopefully as much as the

next person.

(what a shame.)

once brighter than the sun, the rainbows are burning out one by one.

I tell her I will say the three words when they come. naturally.

when I am ready. she nods and never says them again herself.

except, maybe when she is drunk and on top. I don't mind.

I think I will fall in love again. I do. then she shudders under me

and I shake in the wake of her shuddering. afterward we just lie there.

no one says a word. sleep arrives. the thoughts fade away.

Stockholm Syndrome

There is fresh snow on my windowsill.
At a distance   the mailbox
                                                           sits empty as
                                                           my thoughts.

I stand at the door,   solitary,
waiting for the mailman to deliver a parcel
which will shield my cellphone from a *fall*.
A psychopath has locked the woman *he loves* in a glass cage on a
TV show on the TV no one watches anymore,
except maybe these same psychopaths
with women *they love* locked in their homes.

Who am I to witness all this which is not
happening outside my two eyes?
This world so different when I don't see it;
when will it get through this pearl-thick skull
that which I don't see has not happened to my mind
but has still happened *no matter*
what I tell myself.

My bank balance stares at me from this same blue
screen on which I find myself writing.
Makes me wonder, which is truer,
my empty bank account
or these electric worlds from which I am borrowing.
Which is to say if one is a lie
the other cannot be true too
(or at least this is what I ~~need to~~ tell myself).

So here I am
again to find myself captive in my own mind
like everyday

and like everyday to somehow find myself falling in love with this failing self.
My therapist would not say it, but I am doctor enough to
point to a Stockholm *victim* when I see one.
Is it just me
or maybe all of us—
this blue whale of a generation trapped in the glory hole of self-love—suffers this
same syndrome.

Today, *in defeat*, I steal a rose from my father's garden *to present myself.*
Tomorrow, in a bigger hell of *victimhood* and *self-love*, someone might steal a gun.

NOTES

In "*Salam. I Am Sorry for Yesterday,*" *Allah Hafiz* refers to *goodbye* in the Muslim culture. Literally translating from Arabic to English, *Allah Hafiz* becomes *God be your Protector.*

In *"Courage: Making Sure with My Actions That My Mother Knows Her Prayers Don't Work,"* *Haram* means *forbidden* or *proscribed by Islamic law.*

Jai-Namaz means the prayer mat used by Muslims all over the world for prayer five times a day.

In "A Sickness That Is Absolute," *Eid al-Adha* (Feast of the Sacrifice) means what is called in Indian and Pakistani culture *Badi Eid,* or Big Eid, while *Eid al-Fitr* (Feast of Breaking the Fast) is called *Choti Eid,* or Little Eid.

"Basta" at its core refers to the tradition among kids of Jammu and Kashmir, where they kiss a book and then take it to their forehead whenever they have accidentally dropped a book or touched it with their feet. It is considered the sincere way of apologizing to the book.

In "Riptides of You," *Nabood* (نابود) refers to the Persian word for *inexistent* and *Mawjud* (موجود) refers to the Persian word for *existing.*

In "Meditations," *Burqa* means a long, loose garment covering the whole body from head to feet. *Naqaab* means a veil.

In "Some Questions from a Past Self to the Present Self," *schadenfreude* refers to the German word for *joy from pain.*

In "A Juneberry Plant Doesn't Blossom in June," the couplet in Hindi "मेरे लफ़्ज़ों की गहराई मेरी बीमारी नहीं, क्या मेरी बीमारी मेरे लफ़्ज़ों की गहराई है?" translates to *The depth in my words is not my disease, but is my disease the depth in my words?* The same couplet is repeated in Urdu as well:

میرے الفاظ کی گہرائی میری بیماری نہیں
کیا میری بیماری میرے الفاظ کی گہرائی ہے؟

You still live for something when you live for grief. A flood washes away a city and yet some of the trees stand. A river cuts through its shore and yet we crave the noise. A sea brings the beach all its dirt and yet we love the view.

Why not raise a toast for the *unpopular* today. The friendless Jackal. The despised Raccoon. The feared Squirrel. The unloved **you.**

Why not *not* mind what anyone says: the name-calling, the travesties, the allegations, the bullying, the abuse.

Why not, today, just remember this:
*We need you. We need you. **We need you.***

At the Crossroads I Met a Beast

and the beast said, *"You are a museum."*

I asked, *"Museum of what?"*

"A museum of mirrors," he answered.

"What do they see in those mirrors?" I inquired.

"Dreams, half dead, wearing masks of beasts like me, what else?"

"So an unrealized dream is what makes us act like monsters; is this what you're saying?"

*"Look around. Every killer has slaughtered a few dreams before reaching for
and strangulating that first windpipe."*

"I don't want to be a murderer," I whispered, my voice ever-frightened.

"Then don't kill your dreams," the beast replied.

ABOUT THE AUTHOR

Akif Kichloo is an India-born poet currently residing in Montpelier, Vermont. After completing medical school in 2013, he worked in the field of anesthesiology and critical care and then in emergency medicine before giving it all up to write poetry. Akif's poetry transcends all barriers of nationality, language, race, sex, and religion because of its universal nature, each poem signifying something profound about the human experience. While still eating shoelaces, he is currently pursuing an MFA (Writing & Publishing) at Vermont College of Fine Arts.

akifkichloo.com
Twitter: @akifkichloo
Instagram: @akifkichloo
Facebook: @akifkichloo
Tumblr: akifkichloo.tumblr.com
Pinterest: @akifkichloo
Roposo: @akifkichloo